Juniata County

poems by

Thomas Patterson

Finishing Line Press
Georgetown, Kentucky

Juniata County

Copyright © 2017 by Thomas Patterson
ISBN 978-1-63534-202-4 First Edition
All rights reserved under International and Pan-American Copyright Conventions.
No part of this book may be reproduced in any manner whatsoever without written permission from the publisher, except in the case of brief quotations embodied in critical articles and reviews.

ACKNOWLEDGEMENTS

Some of the poems in Juniata County first appeared in the following journals (sometimes in slightly different form):

"Cocoon," "Summering at the Rossers, Roaring Spring," "Ravensbrük Dissociative," and "Room With a View" (*Nimrod International Journal*).
"Because, 1944" (*New Orleans Review*).
"Juniata, 1943" (*Cavalier Literary Couture*).
"The Truth" (as "The Truth, 1943", *Diner*).
"War Games, Roaring Spring" (as "Boy With Balsa Gliders, Roaring Spring", *Hawai'i Pacific Review*).
"Altoona Works" (*Chiron Review*).
"Childhood's End, 1956, Juniata" (as "Two Kinds of Childhood Dark", *Tiger's Eye*).

Publisher: Leah Maines

Editor: Christen Kincaid

Cover Art: Thomas Patterson, from author's personal family collection

Author Photo: Thomas Patterson, from author's personal archive

Cover Design: Elizabeth Maines McCleavy

Printed in the USA on acid-free paper.
Order online: www.finishinglinepress.com
also available on amazon.com

Author inquiries and mail orders:
Finishing Line Press
P. O. Box 1626
Georgetown, Kentucky 40324
U. S. A.

Table of Contents

Juniata, 1943 1

Juniata Generational, 1918-2008 3

War father war, Altoona 6

Barbara Dear 8

Cocoon 10

Eyes 11

War Games, Roaring Spring 12

Summering at the Rossers, Roaring Spring 14

The Girl from Port Royal 15

Altoona Works 16

Hollidaysburg Forest 17

Because, 1944 18

Ravensbrük Dissociative 19

Juniata News 20

The Truth 21

Room with a View 22

Dark Passages, 1952-2008 23

Childhood's End, 1956, Juniata, ... 26

*For my brother and sister,
and
for Garth and Jenny*

Juniata, 1943

Nothing, he thought, above the truth of their burned arms
scarred by the furnace shield of yellows, blues, and greens,
nothing above the lost hope of their glistening backs and shoulders
turned like anvils against the sun
and grandfather, driving home, out of the Juniata train yards
wondering if things might have been different if they'd waited
just a little longer before they married
even a year because then it might all have
been different; sometimes it felt as though his life had meant
nothing at all;
behind the chain-link fence the workmen flicker by
their faces blurring their melting metal eyes
already becoming a part of the past;

his son, sitting on the Lakemont Park
curbing, looks up to see the Octopus cars, on iron tentacles
tumble like forgotten stars
their coronas the waving hair of nine sweet girls, swung
into the blackness by the great geared wheels;

he'll pick out the one he doesn't want to forget
and then one day they'll marry

and then he'll work
like his father aligning the coupling plates
inside the cylinder housing
and fire the steel ovens for the rails;
one night, he'll drive home past the ballpark
down Front Street and by the Cathedral of the
Blessed Sacrament and to the third floor tenement;

he'll walk down the hall to the bedroom where
her voice will be down to a whisper
her throat closed like a blocked tunnel
he'll lie next to her in the dark and wonder
what the end will be like and from
outside, the fireflies in the wind will whisper
into the room

he'll picture her then
in the same spinning car
and that will seem to fit
he'll see her head thrown back and that will seem so perfect;
she'll seem, as then, a languid
curved and quartered moon, lifting,
lifting into the darkness above him

nothing, he'll think
above the truth of that Juniata night
nothing above the truth of her black hair
falling
against a black planet.

Juniata Generational, 1918-2008

Of 2008, my father seeming so far away surrendering
his hold on my hand the spar he clung to
down beneath sleep speaking from a dark lake
and then gone into the
generations

    each one an amalgam of those gone before
giving to all those following their years behind
giving to them their years to come such as 1956
a jar of fireflies with burnished autumn leaves
and clover for their blankets
and six holes punched in the lid so they might breathe
of Barbara's fireflies of Barbara's only
protecting the jar from us and yet holding it out to us
because before she had nothing
and all at once she had everything
after only three only three
of 1918 twenty-seven years before she was born
of the house on 7th Avenue
of grandfather reading "Armistice Signed" in the
Juniata Tribune of 1918
of he and of the summer porch
of the empty wicker chairs rocking in the wind
as though set in motion by ghosts from the past
of the summer birds wheeling back and forth
the grey clouds standing overhead hovering like a pall
like the 1918 a pall so many died
so many never came home leaving themselves
as an offering to the rest of us of the same year Barbara
the same the 1956 two years before our brother
studied the science of the heavens
and learned about the stars beyond the known stars

positing their existence
leaning from the railing wondering of his own deep
and the deep of what he knew of stars and how he
loved those stars
of 1958 and why he knew the deep of stars why he knew
of this leaning
his eyes like our father's eyes our father's of deep blue
of 1944 of our father's plane The Dreamer of its silver wings
striking at the sun
of the children on the ground

of all those children of Polesti and of Nimes
belonging to their fate
as much as though
they were his own children as though in their
convergence with him in that place and time they were his own
and of their asking why
as one would ask a father, why father why—
and he never forgetting those children
concealed in the secret snow
dreaming of them night after night

and never forgetting them night into morning and so he came home and
never spoke of them again
because he had to forget if he wanted to begin living again
and so from that day on
it was as though they had never been born

as of the grey the same grey clouds folding over the red sky
folding over the 1918 on grandfather's porch
folding over Dorothy the Dorothy "of influenza"
died of "not natural" when she was
two, of not natural

of grandmother Virginia kneeling
of almost falling

wanting forever in that moment
to die to be with her darling
her beloved

of asking God to give Dorothy back
knowing it could not be but yearning for it to be

of stumbling
of kneeling

of the grey clouds folding over
and the portal closing

to all that binds us together.

War father war, Altoona

Mother's gone down to the garden
she's forgotten why she went out
the lillies are strangling her roses
which don't seem to belong there at all

the hospital admin's on the wire
from Mercury 0457
they've found her a room at the end of the hall
where nothing can hurt her again

a diminishing grey shore at the window
outside are the stranded the lost
lock up the catch and lower the blinds
war father
war

you came home and couldn't remember
the words we needed to hear
but how could words possibly matter
now the world's run red with blood

will they bring mother by today

how will brother and sister get on

outside

the dead rise in shadow

curling into my room

breathing again softly in whispers

the musk

of an infant perfume

but the darkness believes only in darkness

war

father

war

Barbara Dear

Mother called to you,

Barbara dear, come to the kitchen, see what I've done
standing on the countertop icycool, a knife
pointed down toward the imagined muddy Juniata and the pale awful fish
below; not knowing what words might have saved her
she stabbed at the cold wobbly thing and bathed her legs in blood;

father drove her out to Dixmont right away,

he had to leave her there, this time for good; she waited
in the corner of the room, triangulated
with those coming toward her; afterwards,
he went outside and buried his head in his hands
an ache imprisoned in his throat;

this house is always empty,

the lady who reads to us is gone—
our father's left to visit the sick—or somewhere else—
it's not our business—there's no one to see your resonant, flighty arabesque
performed for the dark mirror in your room
ecarte, leg strongly to the second position,

maybe someone in the imagined crowd is waiting;

your own son seems invincible
your daughter stunning, ochre-skinned
there was another girl
a pastel pink one
but somethng terrible happened;

that tree is teeming with November birds

a few gather at your feeder for anything you have left to give;
you've seen a sleek red cardinal twice
his feet are crippled from a desperate plunge for food
which in the end he was never able to get to

and so he never brought anything home

after that his life was never the same

god, how you love him.

Cocoon

We were the light and the magic
remembered by one winter's day
the gloves on the register stiffened
the wet socks hissed at the door,

again to the measureless yard
the boundary of all that mattered
the work of the day and the dusk
the arc of our ice cocoon,

in the house they have have whispered
"her sadness can never be healed
"they've sent her to Dixmont asylum"
words with no meaning at all,

we tendered the snow into ice-clouds
the clouds into three bright ships
one each for the snow maiden's daughters
who came for us year after year,

their lips were crimson berries
their gowns were crepe de chine
they sparkled like star-lit water
against the April air,

the sun hammered hard at our tower
the wind blew away the door
our lace dome folded to springtime
and died in the summer lawn,

I have the brown eyes of my mother
my sister has her brave dark hair
my brother dreams of a heaven
where the helpless and the lost have gone.

Eyes

In the roundhouse yard where he works at trains
the real trains
grandfather's eyes
fire back heat they get
from hammered rails like the
ovens glow when the lighted wire whitens and goldens cracking
the Mt. Etna furnace
flow

but then he's home next after that when it lets out and he comes down
to where I am
to play I always use the chase and
ball for our first thing
and then if he can
the chase and catch the dog his eyes
cloud a little if you look into them when you're pressed
up close against him after the day goes dark
in the living room
his eyes are
like fireflies' bellies going soft his eyes
are like
fireflies not getting up the last time they go into the grass
because they're going down there and going to die there

the fireflies gather in close against each other
that's how they are
keeping warm now because
starlight is cold

I still look for those eyes in the grasses
the next time and the time after that but I can't find anything like them
anywhere ever again.

War Games, Roaring Spring

This space is for the time of jagged teeth
falling into sprockets of the wheeled watch at once
spinning, whirling, tiring out;
one day to dry up, lock, and stop;

then, shoulders of geared clouds fleece-gauzed
the sky handled lustrous milk, spilled to dull blue bulbs
against the planes sent to rest rocking on green pins
each aimed carefully at reckoned stars;
here's a row of six he's sent crashing, ducking down in infamy
at St. Mere Eglise;
a hundred men fell out—
no leader left—one toppled to the ground
his two metal legs bound into iron rust
trudging through the muck toward the beach
streaming into the pillowed dusk;

he knew the cities, towns, topography
having learned them from his father's navigation maps
so they all dropped out the doors of balsa gliders
just the way it must have happened
and they quickly caught upside down in the trees;

he made them tumble, untangle
from the branches of the beeches
he made them find each other, improvise, survive
unhitching the long trains of their chutes;
allowing them to find what they were looking for—
and they wiggled toward a nest of turret guns made out of sticks;

only until the screen door bounced into the jamb-catch hard
only until then—the clock has carefully slowed and narrowed,

grandmother's come along the walk

like a proven theorem
her lips, as soft as cotton, have muffled every sound;
the weakened sprockets have caught and tightened
like the works of rusted guns

they've given up

the summer's planes run down.

Summering at the Rossers, Roaring Spring

The year we learned what being brother and sister meant
they dropped us off at the Rossers
we walked toward the front door lowering our heads, believing
we had done something wrong
the gate rail bent backward, a fearsome gothic thing

the trees were filled with summer birds
the sparrow weaker than the crow

the creek had as its future the long funnel
washing into the dry bed mouth—

you kept a picture of our mother in your pocket
called "sisters, 1942"—she's wading in the river
pale arms around Aunt Veda's shoulders
the dusk building behind them seemed a great hawk's quilted
wings

the smoke from two cigarettes blossomed in our lungs
down in the fort we built beneath
the coal bin in just one week's time

you took hold of my hand and we left that place
running from darkness into darkness
delivered from the people who pretended to care

ahead, the Juniata River ran toward
the gilded valley of the Sesquehanna, carrying its stories
of girls-in-waiting and their ruined dreams
of boys come home from LeTeil, Polesti and the Saar
numbed into silence

its own tiny arc of love and loss

its histories were our own.

The Girl from Port Royal

On the day her eyes revealed all of their tenderness
she was done with holding back
but who was left to care

she's probably forgotten about the night of mighty stars
or maybe
she never saw it that way in the first place

what really mattered then was the noire reveal of
the pouting curve of her mouth and the spell of
its web of darkness

tough to be fifteen and all ga ga
and some more experienced guy in uniform comes
walking toward you to take possession—man against boy, so then
that's that—

she might have met him the summer before—right after he enlisted
and never mentioned him;
before they say a word to one another I'll walk away—
I won't give either one the satisfaction—

and anyway I'll find someone else next summer
who will be just as good or probably
I'll love her even more

check out those ragged stars riding up against the pale moon
striking down into the blacknesss

they fear nothing and no one.

Altoona Works

He's not thinking of the fierceness of the ovens
(the fireflies like tiny pearls of regret...)
or of the fire-sparked ingot forced against the anvil,
(are lowering into the grasses...)
but of what he has to leave behind instead;
(their paper bellies lighting, dimming...)
he's wondering if it will mean anything to man or to God
(the females whispering...)
that in the roundhouse in the passenger car building
(we're here...we're waiting...)
next to the planning mill, night into morning
(our eggs are tiny stars...)
he forces the coupling pin down, uniting the running stock
(breathing, breathing...)
giving his lean, sinewy back against steel
(into the dew and the dark...)
as an offering to earth and heaven.

Hollidaysburg Forest

I'll go crazy if I don't
find my way out of these woods it's impossibly
dank one tree
looks the same
as another it's easy to lose your
way in this place
it is her voice inside the darkness or concealed in shrouds of green
fern spurs
everybody will someday say the same thing—she was too young
to die and these new voices will be young voices, perhaps
of your own children, and they know what a ripped-out heart
feels like no matter what anyone says about
the young being naïve about what love means

I started out just to go into the cleansing
deep of oak,
spruce, sassafrass
to fall into the blizzard of the forgiving henna dusk

in the regeneration of evening vespers the sweet light of fierce
language
becomes the salvation of truth

it becomes the language of ancestral ghosts asking for a second
chance
to put everything right

they speak and through them
we all speak

Because, 1944

Because they are ready, the blood red cotoneaster
berries, dry blue hydrangea blossoms wilted stiffly
down, place marked out, plat assigned
chisel worked strictly into stone, with Squadron 481
as an ending to the whole thing as though someone's
come from somewhere to read only that

read nothing that came before that because before that
he turned his face to try not see himself
down there, because
his back is to you because he is like a dear house
breaking apart into which no woman will ever go
again

because the sun's in the wrong place because
he looks a terrible mess
because the bandage flopping closed and open
on his right eye he imagines is because the wind has pushed
the Bastogne snowfall into his face because the
golden bullet lodged in his back that he thinks
will send him home
someone has grabbed hold of with the bullet forceps
but he won't go home really because
it can't come out that way because it
won't.

Ravensbrük Dissociative

The garden roses loved you and they trembled
as though your fingers brushed against
each crimson throat,

smooth clouds warned carefully, *verboten*
wondering if you would ever come back
and why you left with Nessa when she said it was time to go

down through the tunnel under the house
out into the mirrored darkness, broken in two
by searing stars;

right away the Kapo asked you to agree, *ja*
that your yellow hair meant nothing, *ja*
that your blue eyes were a lie;

it all began the day you stepped down *auf der strasse*
practicing a cabriole learned at the academy—
the street was sunlit then—yet how could that be—

weren't you already there when the guard led Nessa
toward the group of newly inspected women
and then pointed to you,

kommen hier zu mir—
ending with a glib
das ist das—

after that you heard nothing
saw nothing
wanted nothing again;

every moment it feels that you will stumble
falling down into the funnel of damp air
a lonely child again in abba's garden
looking up through the cylinder of darkness
into the lip of the stars that might save you
dreaming their shapes into distances.

Juniata News

The dining room lampshade is trembling
but it's probably just the house settling—
I can't get you out of my mind anymore
since you've decided not
to remember me—
the boys wrote home about
a plane coming in at Odna
rolling dangerously sideways
against the targeted bridge
another B-24 taken off the board
in the headaquarters map room—
this changed predicted scenarios—

cousin Linda is brushing out her hair in the
parlor sunroom bending over at the waist getting at it
from underrneath where its thickness
gathers together the spun gold
unhusked spilling down onto the floor beside me
what a wicked crush I have on her—

all the Joe's running in onto Utah Beach
off the Higgens ramp into a sky strewn with vertical fire
where on earth did they get the courage for that—

dad's been home since January he thinks
it doesn't fit that he's come back when so many didn't
make it; he says it's a mistake that he's still alive
he looks at us tongue-tied chewed up inside
the words he wants to say crash up on a pathway
out of his throat
at night in his dreams the boys he loved
adorned in their crimson plumage
fall out of the sky like stricken birds.

The Truth

The truth is in the cold-rolled steel turned hard against the anvil
riveted into the trestle, on its back in broad combed muscle
beats the belly of serpentine track;

the truth is in the roundhouse
cable wound through copper,
power-forged in the turret-cab
where the firebox spills flint
down below the rail
running hard to the eastern mouth;

the truth is in the troop cars in at Altoona station
the first leg to Betio
where Tarawa's back will be broken
up along the revetment
and on to the red blind beach;
the truth is in the many ways that arms will be caught in wire and feet
shrug in camouflaged netting winched aft down a Higgens boat

the truth is in the Hoyer lift
tracking from hallway to bedroom
where they've tucked you under the blankets
in the silly, languorous dusk

the truth is wound in her black hair, perfumed
tangled, undone

the truth that no longer matters

once burned in your belly like a fifty

laid down by a pillbox gun.

Room with a View

This is how you remember walking down the pavement
one Sunday evening late in September
8th Street to Frontz's Pharmacy and back again;
there is a bag you saw last night
that has ended up blown into a corner
from which there is no escape;
this is the *Altoona Mirror* declaring,
"Allies Roll into France"
opened on grandfather's lap;
here is the summer unleafing to autumn
the blue aster on the porch the last to be doomed;
down the avennue is your mother's new home
the inside numb as a polished white corridor;
this is a town where your father once lived
the ballpark a mirage the players a dream;
these were the bells, Emanuelle
of Parisse Notre Dame du Rhone
tolling the beginning of liberation;
this was your father's plane, *The Dreamer*,
coming back in flak-blacked two engines feathered
skidding across the wet tarmac;
these were the children on the bridge at Nimes
playing at la marelle ronde
stumbling to the ground;
here is the hallway below the landing
where the iris are closing fall after fall
stiffening and darkening,
a prelude to forgiveness;
here is a room you walked back into
looking for something you must have lost
here at this window you dreamed as a child
earth moon and stars
in perfect confluence.

Dark Passages, 1952 - 2008

2008

The hands of someone who loved us someone we never knew are folded
on the bodice of her summer dress she and her dress completed in
all their uses conveyed into a dark passage of blues yellows golds
the husked silk of her skin terribly humbled

1952

I have lowered the seat-back down and gone underneath to the
floor on Pennsy 1651 build date 1928 out of commission date 1968
crawling near the nylon
stockinged feet of the ladies who smell like fresh washed hair
hoping that one may be chosen to be our new mother

my brother and sister have found the baggage car and
opened the most promising cases trying to cover up
what's become of us by dressing in other children's
clothes a game we play over and over

the rail has cracked
somewhere between Logan Valley and Roaring Spring
we've come to a standstill
the woman in the blue dress
who my sister will always remember once died
where we eventually start back up

2006

my brother is trying to find me
someone he knew died young
but something of love he said
had been accomplished

our sister is watching the robin near the feeder in her yard
he returns every morning with his broken leg pointing sideward
if he could go back to two summers ago he might discover a way not
to tumble from the wire to the branch to the pavement
and then maybe he would be young again and whole again

2008

the endgame of our father's suffering is cued by mundane
calamaties: forgetting why he walked across the quad to
his apartment
designated "Assisted Living" and
discontinuing letter writing because the word that should
begin the next sentence
cannot be retrieved

I've taken him out of the Florida home where they'll keep him
until he dies; I've signed him out until 9 tonight

we're driving south now down through Palatka
pretending we won't go back
our silhouettes merging in the sun's bright fires
bringing us closer than we've ever been before

we've stopped at the Route 1 Café for a bite to eat
all at once he's tired again and wants to go

his walker parked in the corner is a bright chrome death machine
reminding him of something to do with the war

he's looking at the numbers at the bottom of the check
but they've somehow morphed into a gaggle of impotent
worms
one curling around the other

I've taken his hands into my hands

his skin has turned purple because of angio sarcoma

his blue eyes are two hopeless balloons

they look

but do not see

I cannot save him now

as he was never able to save me

yet something of love has been accomplished

here in this place

that for him

never existed

I have felt tenderness

for a wounded brother.

Childhood's End, 1956, Juniata

The garden was blooming in front and back like blown silk
                the war long over;
      the nights were summer hot and blanched crimson
with leaves floating in near-evening
we outgrew the clustered dusk
        the organic rind of purple veins that held us close
the sweet husk of a mother's breast
  day after day we left
        into the bare alleyways—they offered their secret arms
under a rusting sun
the flireflies lit quickly, incandescently
          compressed in time and
        left behind thin light from their green and yellow sheathing
            to write their histories near us on the grass
        lifting and falling and trembling once
           bright on a leaf
                  the leaflet trembling back

hands of rain swept on the throats of roses
        and on the lillies' mouths
we pushed through the forbidden fences
we bellied-up on ripe tomatoes in the soaked shed floor
split with seedy walls the cool syrup sliding down our throats

the phantom darkness
took hold when dull light fell

inside our houses the mothers left behind read sleepily at bedroom lamps
      dreaming and
           holding one another's hands in silence

they walked exquisite nights in exotic cities far away
and their jewels glistened on the floors and the night clicked
      off and on

our fathers feared their quickened restless breathing
as the age of complacency fears the age to come

finished with this time and place the moths were diaphanous
        and full of weakness

we ran down against all darkness
                all calling back
from doors and doomed earthen walkways
down another
        deeper further faster
                outrunning our coming dark
                      drunk with one last summer.

Additional Acknowledgements

Special thanks to Colette Jonopulos and to Francine Ringold for their great care in the reading and review of this manuscript and their helpful edits and suggestions.

Thanks to James Cronin, fellow poet, for his support, advice, and encouragement.

Author's Note

Many of the locations in this collection are in Blair County, Juniata, Altoona, Pennsylvania; The title, "Juniata County" reflects the importance of the proximity of these areas with the Juniata River, and the musicality and beauty of the name itself; the collection is a work of imagination and not a historical document; any reader familiar with Blair will no doubt recognize some of the landmarks in the poems.

Thomas Patterson lives in Westport, Massachusetts. He is retired from his work as a School Adjustment Counselor/ crisis counselor in the Fall River School Department and as an Instructor in English at Bristol Community College, where he taught composition and literature. His most recent poetry appears in *Nimrod International Journal,* *The South Carolina Review,* *New Orleans Review,* *CutBank,* and *Chiron Review.*

His work appears in 50 journals and periodicals and he has had work nominated for the Pushcart Prize. He is a graduate of Northeastern University, receiving a Master of Arts in English and a graduate of Rhode Island College, earning an MEd in Counseling.

www.ingramcontent.com/pod-product-compliance
Lightning Source LLC
LaVergne TN
LVHW051614080426
835510LV00020B/3281